LEADERSHIP

REACHING OUT, PULLING UP, HOLDING ON, TO STAND STRONG TOGETHER

THOMAS J. SNEE, M.ED

MINDSTIR MEDIA

LEADERSHIP!

**A *Balance* in the…
Sharing & Receiving
of Ideas and Actions for All,
through**

VALUES!

Thomas J. Snee, M.Ed.

TABLE OF CONTENTS

THE AUTHOR'S TAKE

GREETINGS, *AND* **THANK YOU** *to all who are reading this book!* It has been well over two years since my last two books, *You Raise Me Up* and *What's Up, Life?* were published. In this book, I would just like to share some of my own thoughts and experiences from those who inspired me to be a *leader,* starting with my journey in the U.S. Navy, as a middle school classroom teacher/administrator, in the halls of Congress, until now. My only desire is to give back, share, and continue to make a difference from my past *leadership* experiences.

So, exactly what is *leadership?* Many have defined it as a desired destiny to action. Much has been written and observed from its purpose to be an inspirational movement of their ***own*** courses of actions, or a way of life, as it was for me. In some disciplines, the term *leadership* has perhaps been overrated or has even been hazardous to good order of common sense. Hopefully, it will be further defined as *"a posture of goodwill and motivation to a more positive and productive course of action."*

Fundamentally, it is human nature from one's own conscience. *Leadership* has been studied, discussed, and even discharged by many who are already great and successful *leaders.* Their impactful legacies have produced giant gains that have *initiated, guided, and served others* from an already impetuous self-ownership, that fostered a masterful reinforcement by all accounts and measurements, an acceptable balance, or simply, basics of conscience.

For my visual partners on the subject, please permit me to point out some humbling variances as described in the *Empowerment* chapter of *The Amish Boy*. The picture is simple and culturally enriched, to a meaning of an *already developed, tested framework of woven standards,* defining a magnitude called *leadership.*

The setting subscribes to confidence and a comfort zone within *the classroom of a life of cultural and social unity*. The young person standing, with a hand positioned firmly on the desk, will only produce the fabric of a futuristic design for its potential composition. That *person*, male or female, hails from an already well-grounded acceptance of culture and persona from their humble labors.

Like *YOU,* it will attest to a personal trait of merit from a rich continuum of clarity, a well-established set of guidelines, mentoring, and courage to serve as benchmarks from its *teacher, coach, mentor*, and *encourager*. Yes, the *encourager.* These provide life's values in resourcing and reasoning to further embrace a shared acceptance of actions from solid social practices. On the teacher's desk are the poignant health and environmental foods of life: an apple for nourishment and a plant for growth, producing an inner dependence for times ahead.

The chalkboard will be the mantel for future expressions of ideas and ideals. It extends to both *the learned* and *the learner's* fullest potential. Cultures and environments co-exist and articulate a shared partnership to the first step. Not perfect, but a rich and cooperative inquiry into future progress. When *goals* are set, *steps* lead to productive objectivity from its very grassroots. If *goals* are not met, one only needs to rediscover and replant another set of *steps* for the needed outcomes. *Goals* are the capstones from self-rooted *steps* of achievements.

Thus, you have total *leadership*. Remember, risks need to be tested: **"Amateurs built the Ark; Professionals built the Titanic."** Stature, determination, and unification always equate to the simplest task to a solid movement of success and mobility. Once *learned* with the *learner*, a solid, cooperative, thumbprint of inspiration will be achieved by the *leader.*

Within this book, I have highlighted the letters from the word

LEADERSHIP to spell out my shared ideas and ideals for each chapter. A collaborative engagement, to promote a steady path for *You,* the reader, to follow with purpose. Perhaps an *"inspiration towards a forward movement"?* My only hope again is that it will inspire *You* to take the next step: **Lead** people and *manage* systems. You have the will, desire, and drive…now just do it! *You just need to* ***BE BOLD, CARING, DARING, HUMBLE, STRONG, A SERVANT LEADER, and BE YOU! NOW GO OUT AND LEAD!***

Tom :)

IN GRATITUDE AND DEDICATION!

I just want to take a moment and say THANK YOU and to dedicate this book to all of you: my family, classmates, shipmates, mentors, leaders, and students, from the bottom of my heart. You truly have been my EPICENTER to success. Yes, there are many more, but in writing this book, you stood by me with your **encouragement, guidance, words, and mentorship** *to* **press on!** *Throughout my many years, you have always given me the right 'rudder order' and 'speed' to steer the course to come alongside and* **lead***!* <u>THANK YOU!</u>
FLTCM(SW) Richard P. O'Rawe, USN, (Ret); LCDR Rod Elish, USN, (Ret); CWO4 Mark Cortor, USCG, (Ret); CWO3 Bruce R. Collins, USN, (Ret); CWO2 James T. Trautz, Jr., USN, (Ret); CNOCM (SW) Harry J. Kantrovich, USN, (Ret), EdD; and HTCS (SW) Alan Marcotte, USN, (Ret)

*****

For my students, "Don't give up, you got this, now lead"!
You may be shy, quiet, sit in the back row, struggle academically or in sports, socially distant, rejected, and ignored, but I get it. I have been there too. This book is about **YOU**. <u>YOU CAN DO IT</u>*!* **You** *are respected, valued, and recognized. The world is waiting for* **YOU TO LEAD**. *Giving from the heart, in acts of kindness and conscience, is the way to go!* **DON'T GIVE UP!** *We need* **YOU***! As a teacher,* **YOU** *have* **'raised me up through inspiration.'** <u>THANK YOU!</u>

**BE STRONG, BE BRAVE, BE BOLD, BE HUMBLE,
BUT ALWAYS HAVE COURAGE and JUST BE YOU!**

FOREWORD FROM THE 'MASTERS'

FIRST MET TOM SNEE MORE years ago than I remember. I was a young sailor and Tom was a seasoned sailor who entered the Navy in 1965, fifteen years before me. I was a college graduate, married, and had five years in business management before I enlisted. I cannot remember the exact year or the command I was at when I met Tom. But, from that first day, I knew I was in the presence of a leader, and a man in whose footsteps I would hope to follow. He did not hesitate to ask me about my life and experiences in business, the Navy thus far, marriage, and my thoughts on what made a good leader. That was my first confirmation of Tom's leadership; he wanted the perspective of others.

We have stayed in contact through Tom's years as a Force Master Chief at Commander, Navy Recruiting Command, and a Veteran's Advocate for Fleet Reserve Association, a middle school teacher, and as the twelfth Executive Director for Fleet Reserve Association, where he served 60,000 staff and members of the organization. Servant leadership was always at Tom's forefront.

This is Tom's third book. His first came from the challenge of one of his former middle school students, who at the time was studying at Boston University. Just as with the many sailors he touched, his students never forgot Tom. Thank you to my shipmate, friend, and mentor of many years for trusting me with this honor of writing your book foreword.

Harry J. Kantrovich, Ed.D.
CNOCM (SW), USN, (Ret)

*****

There have been literally THOUSANDS of books written about leadership throughout the years, but writing ABOUT leadership and BEING a leader are two completely different things.

I once was told, "Leaders lead people, managers manage things." But what I have learned over the years is that TRUE leaders are that magical combination of both, as well as a mixture of teacher, coach, advisor, and mentor as well. They have the strength and presence to command, yet the ability to follow. They have the authority to direct, but a willingness to listen. They teach, but they are always learning, and they GLADLY pass on the lessons they have learned to the next generation.

This is more than a definition of leadership – it is the character of my friend of thirty-plus years, Tom Snee.

Tom is fond of telling our friends, our families, and our shipmates that I have been one of his mentors. But, ironically, it is me who has been the student all these years, and my friend is too humble to admit it.

You want the definition of a leader? There it is. Someone who leads people and manages things. Someone who teaches, coaches, advises, and mentors. And yes, someone humble enough to defer credit to the next generation.

To Tom, thank you, my friend – you are the epitome of a leader and I will forever be in your debt!

James T. Trautz, Jr.
CWO2, USN (Ret.)

*****

Recently, I was honored by being asked to share some thoughts about my longtime friend Thomas J. Snee, NCCM(SW), BS, M.Ed. The question was not where to start, but rather where to stop. Tom and I have been friends since he took a young, angry sailor under his wing. I do not think I was the first and I know that I was not the last. There are hundreds, if not thousands of men and women who have had successful careers thanks to the steady influence of Tom.

Things I have learned from and about Tom. First, Tom is genuinely one of the nicest human beings that I have met in my sixty-plus years. I cannot count the number of young sailors, far from home on a holiday, who were welcomed into the Snee household. Again, I am sure I was not the first and I know I was not the last. We are all familiar with the picture of the person, in a moment of indecision, with a demon whispering in one ear and an angel whispering in the other. For many of us, Tom was that Guardian Angel, quietly suggesting the right course.

Another thing, Tom is Tom. You may be a young sailor, or a middle school student, or senior sailor, or a senior officer, or even an elected official, but Tom is Tom. Everyone, regardless of age or station, gets to see the same calm, jovial, and concerned Tom. I do not think he would make a good actor, and certainly not a good gambler, for he does not have a duplicitous bone in his body. He has been the same genuine Tom since we first met back in the 1970s.

In closing, I would like to touch on the topic of his latest book, *LEADERSHIP*. Tom is a LEADER, not because he wants to lead, but because people want to follow him. His wise counsel has been sought by a wide range of individuals for several years. I am proud to be his friend.

Bruce R. Collins
CWO-3, USN, (Ret)

CHARACTERISTICS OF LEADERSHIP

THOMAS J. SNEE, M.ED.

LEAD: "The development and testing from proven standards and values that, when launched, become a proactive set of cultural and social allegiances, to a desired course of action that can only influence movement."

EMPOWERMENT: "The quality of a leader, from demonstrated personal examples, that permits others to identify, activate, and pursue actions of excellence to fulfill their potential."

AMBITION: "An intrinsic inner force, when featured, that springboards a proven course of positive energy towards a desired point of reference which can only benefit everyone."

DISTRACTORS: "Unsolicited and negative expressions that are directed at another person who otherwise would seek a virtuous and harmonious effort of character towards a peaceful and purposeful potential; they take away from the overall leadership accomplishment from within."

EDUCATORS: "The *mentors and coaches* of the world who seek fundamental networking proficiencies to enhance the needed compatibilities and values to enrich a more fertile cultivation and nurturing harvest in the lives of future learners."

RESPECT: "A recognized set of behaviors from the actions of progressive thinkers, in self-composure, criterions, and critiques, that will channel to an upright character of self-worth and dignity to others."

SELF-CHARACTER & CONFIDENCE: "The authenticity of one's heart, soul, conscience, and spirit that contributes to a solid <u>turf of valor</u>, driven to a profound cause."

HUMILITY: "The *'mirror of life'* when reflecting sincere responsibility and tranquility through efforts affecting another's judgement in their actions."

INSPIRATION: "The captivations of entrusted admirations when observed by others that autonomously become the behavior in others."

POTENTIAL: "That *'One Moment in Time'* when ideas are pursued, actively demonstrated, proven, and achieved in the destinies of future promises."

*"Listen, Love, Mentor, Coach, Let Go, Then
Lead to Actions of Success"!*

*Leadership through Character Defined:
Be Curious, Be Creative, Be Caring and Be Confident*

TEN LESSONS IN LEADERSHIP!

BE CAUTIOUS NOT TO LABEL PEOPLE

Labels placed on people may define your relationship to them and could restrict their full potential.

EVERYONE DESERVES RESPECT

We often and wrongly treat others with less respect than they deserve. Everyone is entitled to and deserves respect.

COURTESY MAKES A DIFFERENCE

Be courteous to everyone, regardless of their status in life. Common courtesies among co-workers help bridge the team. Make your daily words be perfunctory "hellos" as heartfelt greetings to everyone that will make a sincere difference.

TAKE TIME TO GET TO KNOW YOUR PEOPLE

Life and work can be hectic. There are no excuses for not knowing the people who work for and with you.

ANYONE CAN BE A HERO

Do not sell your people short. Any one of them can be the hero who rises to the occasion when duty calls. It is easier to turn to a proven performer when the chips are down, but never ignore the rest of the team. Today's 'rookie' could be tomorrow's 'superstar.'

LEADERS MUST ALWAYS BE HUMBLE

The most modern-day heroes and leaders are anything but humble, especially if your "hero meter" is based on today's athletic fields. End celebrations and self-boasting that we have come to expect from sports greats. Leaders should always be humble.

LIFE WON'T ALWAYS GIVE YOU WHAT YOU THINK YOU DESERVE

We work hard and deserve recognition, right? However, sometimes you just must persevere, even when accolades do not come your way. We do what we do, not for the recognition, but because it is the right thing to do, and it is our trade. Do not pursue glory; pursue excellence.

NO JOB, REGARDLESS, IS EVER BENEATH A LEADER

A leader can do any job with a smile and dignity. No job is ever beneath a leader.

PURSUE EXCELLENCE TO THE END

No matter what life's tasks show you, do them well. Dr. Martin Luther King said, ***"If life makes you a street sweeper, be the best street sweeper you can be."***

LIFE IS A LEADERSHIP LABORATORY

All too often we look to some school or class to be taught leadership when, in fact, life is a ***leadership laboratory***. Those you meet every day teach you enduring lessons, if you just take time to stop, be SILENT, look, and LISTEN. You encounter people every day; learn leadership outreach skills from everyone you meet. Never miss an opportunity to learn from them.

L_{EAD}

"The development and testing of proven standards and values that, when launched, become a proactive set of cultural and social allegiances, to a desired course of action that can only influence movement."

"Leadership is not a science, but a behavioral model in the service to others. Its consequences, whether positive or negative, will depend on the very advocacy of its disciplines in the execution and demonstration to and for others."

Thomas J. Snee, M.Ed.

"Even when obstacles may seem to be overwhelming, the great leader will always improvise, adapt, and overcome."

GMCM Delbert Black, MCPON-1

"Ability takes you to the top, character keeps you there."

George Mason, Statesman, Commonwealth of Virginia

"Winning is not everything—but making the effort to win is."

Vince Lombardi, Football Coast Green Bay Packers

"If you limit yourself, you don't reach your full potential."

Joseph P. Moore

"You would always rather be somewhere other than where you are. When you finally get to where you want to be, don't forget to stop and bask in the moment of where you are."

Joseph P. Moore

"Leadership is a privilege to better the lives of others. It is not an opportunity to satisfy personal greed."

Mwai Kibaki

"Life is a Leadership Laboratory."

Thomas J. Snee, M.Ed.

"<u>Great minds</u> discuss ideas. <u>Average minds</u> discuss events. <u>Small minds</u> discuss people."

Eleanor Roosevelt, First Lady

"Conscience is the most sacred of all properties."

James Madison, 4th President of the United States

"Honest conviction is my courage; the Constitution is my guide."

Andrew Johnson, 17th President of the United States

"A person who feels <u>appreciated</u> will always do more than what is expected."

Anonymous

LEADERSHIP PHILOSOPHY:

S O U L: *"SWAGGER, OWNERSHIP, UNITY, AND LEADERSHIP."*

7 Cs *of a winning team:*

"Culture, Contagious, Consistency, Communication, Connect, Commitment, and Caring."

"A <u>Contribution</u> *is ok, but a* <u>Commitment</u>, *is a lifelong achievement of memories from an established legacy."*

Thomas J. Snee, M.Ed.

"Strive for <u>progress</u>, *not* <u>perfection</u>*."*

"Channel your <u>passions</u> *and your* <u>future</u> *towards a positive sustainability!"*

"You can't solve your problems with old ideas."

"You can't walk backwards into the future."

"HEALTH isn't just what you're EATING. It's what you're THINKING and what you're SAYING."

"Sometimes the best thing that you can do is not Think, Wonder, Imagine, or be Obsessed. Just **BREATHE** *and have faith that everything will work out for the best.* <u>The definition of PATIENCE!</u>"*

SO-SHARE-THIS

"Morale is when your <u>hands and feet</u> *keep on WORKING, and your head says,* '<u>it can't be done</u>'."*

ADM Ben Moreell, (CEC), USN,
Founder of the Navy SEABEEs.

"War is not sustainable when you come to know your enemy as a person."

"Train people well enough so they can leave; treat them well enough so they don't want to. Take care of your employees and they will take care of your business. It is as simple as that. LOYAL EMPLOYEES ARE ASSETS – NOT LIABILITIES"!

Richard Branson

"Build a pyramid and it will speak well of others. In the end, it will stand forever from your character and the cornerstone of who you are and its effect on others."

Thomas J. Snee, M.Ed.

"Above all, we should ensure that OUR LIBERTY is not an end in itself, but rather, a means to win respect to HUMAN DIGNITY for all classes in our society."

ADM Hyman Rickover, USN

"People's lives should never be collateral duties over safety."

Thomas J. Snee, M.Ed.

LESSONS FOR EACH DAY...

"Intelligence is not about <u>knowing everything</u> without questioning, but rather, to question what you <u>think you know, about everything.</u>"

<u>The Five Keys to Legendary Leadership</u>

<u>Hold to the Vision!</u>

Lead *with your mind. Keep seeing in your mind's eye where you are going, especially when nobody else does.*

Build Your People!

Lead *from the heart. Give people something to live up to – something great – and they usually will. The substance of influence is to pull…not push.*

Do the Work!

Lead *from your gut. Stay hugely humble, stay grounded, and get mud on your boots. And trust yourself.*

Stand for Something!

Lead *with your soul. You can lead only as far as you grow. And you will grow only as far as you let yourself.*

Practice Giving Leadership!

Great leadership is never about the leader. Great leadership is about holding people up. The best way to increase your influence is to give it away.

**The SHARING & RECEIVING of Ideas
and Actions to and for All!**

Things money cannot buy…

Manners, Morals, Respect, Character, Common Sense, Trust, Patience, Class, Integrity.

THAT'S NOT MY JOB!

"This is a story about four people, **Everybody, Somebody, Anybody,** *and* **Nobody.**

There once was an important job to be done and <u>Everybody</u> was sure that <u>Somebody</u> would do it. <u>Anybody</u> could have done it, but <u>Nobody</u> did it. <u>Somebody</u> got truly angry about it because it was <u>Everybody</u>'s job. <u>Everybody</u> thought <u>Anybody</u> could do it, but <u>Nobody</u> realized that <u>Everybody</u> would not do it. It ended up that <u>Everybody</u> blamed <u>Somebody</u> when <u>Nobody</u> did what <u>Anybody</u> could have done. The lesson here is that it's <u>EVERYBODY</u>'s job to do it."

"Leadership is not about being in charge. Leadership is about taking care of those in your charge."

"The courage of life is often a less dramatic spectacle than the courage of a final moment. It is not less than a magnificent mixture of triumph and tragedy. People do what they must—despite personal consequences, despite obstacles and dangers and pressures—and that is the basis of all human morality."

John F. Kennedy, 35th President of the United States

"The greatest leader is not necessarily the one who does the greatest things. He is the one that gets people to do the greatest things."

Ronald Reagan, 40th President of the United States

"What do all leaders have in common? They challenge the most out of their crews, which depends on three variables: The leader's needs, the organization's atmosphere, and the crew's potential competence."

"Mediocre leaders never take the trouble to get to know their people."

"Do you know the difference between a **BOSS** *and a* **LEADER**? *A* **LEADER** <u>knows</u> *the way,* <u>goes</u> *the way, and* <u>shows</u> *the way."*

"A <u>DREAM</u> *written down with a date becomes a* <u>GOAL</u>. *A* <u>GOAL</u> *broken down into steps becomes a* <u>PLAN</u>. *A* <u>PLAN</u> *backed by* <u>ACTION</u> *becomes* <u>REALITY</u>."*

"Great LEADERS don't set out to be a LEADER. They set out to make a difference. It is never about the role, it is always about the GOAL."

SET GOALS

Push Yourself

MOVE

DON'T QUIT

NO EXCUSES

Be Awesome

YOU GOT THIS

"Empathy is an internal leadership skill needed today!"

"Your past successes will only be overshadowed by your future successes."

"Success is never owned. It is rented and the rest is due every day."

"Leadership is not a position or title in Life. Rather, it is actions and examples that you show, model, and demonstrate for others."

"Excellence is not a skill, it's an attitude."

"Discipline is not a light switch. Discipline is a way of life."

John Harbaugh, NFL Coach, Baltimore Ravens

"I cannot control the wind, but I can adjust the sail."

"I am not afraid of the storms, for I am learning how to sail my ship."

"A true leader has the confidence to stand alone, the courage to make tough decisions, and the compassion to listen to the needs of others. A leader does not set out to be a leader but becomes one by the equality of his actions and the integrity of his intent."

Douglas MacArthur, General, U.S. Army

"Leadership is not always found in books, manuals, lesson plans, presentations, or slides. When discovered and searched, they just may be sitting right next to us, through the very interactions that we may be having with them, and the others, who are also seeking the same common purpose, to lead."

Thomas J. Snee, M.Ed.

"If you have the courage to begin, then you have the courage to succeed."

"Be the cheerleader in people's lives! It's astounding what people can do when they have someone who believes, cheers, encourages, and loves them!"

"Surround yourself with a team that can help change your perspective. Above all, respect each other as persons of dignity, and can kick butt together."

"Staying connected, we are like anchor chain links. We must stay connected to 'heave around' on THE ANCHOR. We know what the ANCHOR's purpose is and therefore we should be that 'link' that always maintains, holds, and bonds us together as shipmates and SAILORS. STAY CONNECTED! ANCHORS AWEIGH!"

FORCM (SW) Peter T. Yeschenko, USN, (Ret)

"The truth, are my actions."

Anonymous

"The best project you'll ever work on is you."

"Somebody once asked me what I'm going to do when I make it to the top. I said, 'Reach my hand back down to the rest'."

"The measure of a man is what he does with power and control."

Plato

"If serving is below you, leadership is beyond you."

Anonymous

"LEAD FROM THE FRONT."

"Someone Else"

Today we were saddened to learn about the departure of one of our most valued members, **Someone Else. Someone's** *leaving created a vacancy that will be difficult to fill.* **Else** *has been with us for many years, and for every one of those years,* **Someone** *did far more than a normal person's share of the work and was truly respected by all alike; well, almost by most. Whenever there was a job to step into, support that needed showing up for, or a meeting that needed to be attended, one name was on everyone's list –* "Let **Someone Else** *do it." Whenever leadership was mentioned,* **Someone Else** *was over-looked for inspiration as well as results.* **Someone Else** *could have worked with that group but was ignored or rejected. It was common knowledge that* **Someone Else** *was among the most liberal givers at our place. Whenever there was a financial need or fill-in for an event or some insignificant situation, everyone just assumed* '**Someone Else** *would make up the difference.'* **Someone Else** *was a wonderful person, sometimes appearing superhuman but hurting inside. If the truth were known, everybody expected too much of* **Someone Else.** *Now* **Someone Else** *is gone! We wonder now what we are going to do.* **Someone Else** *left a wonderful example to follow, but who is going to follow up or fill in? Who is going to do the things* **Someone Else** *did? So, when* **you** *are asked to help this year, remember, we can't depend on* **Someone Else** *anymore."*

"When you set standards and stick to them, there will be people in your life who will fall away. Let them."

Steve Maraboli

"Leaders lead people; managers manage things and systems."

"You can never go wrong by doing the right thing."

CWO3 James Trautz, USN, (Ret)

"People with integrity do what they say they are going to do. Others make excuses."

Dr. Laura

"Complaining about a problem without posing a solution is called whining."

Teddy Roosevelt, 26th President of the United States

"He who has never learned to obey can never be a good commander."

Aristotle, Philosopher

"<u>Leaders</u> *are creators in their own lives.* <u>Followers</u> *let life happen to them. The* <u>best leaders</u> *not only develop their people, but are advocates for their future."*

"General Eisenhower used to demonstrate the art of leadership with a simple piece of string. He'd put it on the table and say: **Pull it** *and it will follow wherever you wish.* **Push it***, and*

it will go nowhere at all.' It's just that way when it comes to leading people."

"The supreme quality of leadership is integrity."

Dwight D. Eisenhower, 34th President of the United States

"A leadership title is not a position or platform. It is an influence to promote progressive results in its very actions."

Thomas J. Snee, M.Ed.

"Real leadership must be demonstrated by example, not precept."

"Leadership is not a position or title in Life. Rather it is actions and examples you show, model, and demonstrate to others."

"Leadership is not a journey to rise in the ranks. Leadership is a journey to help those around us to rise."

"The measure of a man is what he does with power and control."

Plato

"Leadership is influence towards a desired action."

John C. Maxwell

"To lead is to motivate, guide, and serve others."

"Do your boss's work first, and his boss's work before that."

"One General Officer's bosses would pick up litter and trash as we walked around the Army Post. If the boss did it, then everyone else did it without being ordered to."

"I may manage the team, but I try to lead the players to victory."

Paul Brown, Coach, Cleveland Browns

"You don't need managers. You NEED LEADERS."

Martin Luther King

"A positive attitude causes a chain reaction of positive thoughts, events, and outcomes. It is a catalyst, and it sparks extraordinary results."

Wade Boggs

Empowerment

"The quality of a leader, from demonstrated personal examples, that permits others to identify, activate and pursue actions of excellence to fulfill their potential."

"The world, as viewed from a student's perspective."

Thomas J. Snee, M.Ed.

"Outstanding leaders go out of their way to boost the self-esteem of their personnel. If people believe in themselves, it's amazing what they can accomplish."

Sam Walton

"God gives you the opportunity to be great. It is what you choose to do with it that makes it count for others."

Joseph P. Moore

"I am not in competition with anyone. I have no desire to play their games of being better than anyone. I am simply trying to be better than the person I was yesterday."

The Mind Perceptions

"Never tell people <u>how</u> to do things. Tell them <u>what</u> to do, and they will surprise you with their ingenuity."

George S. Patton, General, U.S. Army

"<u>The best executive </u>is the one who has enough sense to pick good people to do what they want done, and the self-restraint to keep from meddling with them while they do it."

Theodore Roosevelt, 26th President of the United States

"Leadership is the art of giving people a platform for spreading ideas that work."

Seth Godin

"Always, always, the plight of a person is to be expressed."

Thomas J. Snee, M.Ed.

"Ships don't sink because of the water around them; ships sink because of the water that gets in them. Don't let what's happening around you get inside you and weigh you down."

"You will always continue to suffer if you have an emotional reaction to everything that is said to and about you. True power

and control is sitting back and observing things with logic and with restraint. If words control you, that means everyone else can control you. Breathe and allow things to pass."

Warren Buffett

"God gave you a fingerprint that no one else has so you can leave an imprint that no one else can."

"If your actions create a legacy that inspires others to dream more, learn more, do more, and become more, then you are an excellent leader."

Dolly Parton

"Your degree is just a piece of paper; your education is realized in your behavior."

"Listen, learn, and be silent."

"People buy into the leader before they buy into the vision."

John Maxwell

"Leaders must free up their subordinates to fulfill and allow their talents to be manifested to the utmost."

"We should tap the potentials of our people who have never been recognized. Those employees will take prideful ownership."

"Leaders become great leaders, not because of their power, but because of their ability to empower others."

John Maxwell

"Hope can only anchor the soul!"

"Always BE YOU, the person from within."

Thomas J. Snee, M.Ed.

"You can't calm the storm...so stop trying. What you can do is calm yourself. The storm will eventually pass."

"MOTIVATION is not an EXCUSE; it's a MINDSET. CREATE, DEMONSTRATE, and EXHIBIT your PROGRESSIVE GROWTH. MAKE IT SHINE from within you, and for others!"

Thomas J. Snee, M.Ed.

"Just because you are struggling, it doesn't mean you're weak or failing. It just means you have another course to 'sail'!

BE STRONG, BE BRAVE, BE BOLD, BE HUMBLE>>>BE YOU!*"*

"Train your mind to always stay calm in every situation."

"One of the best lessons you can learn in life is to master how to remain calm."

Catherine Pulsiver

*"If You **always** do what you have **always** done, you will **always** be where you have **always** been."*

"Avert misunderstanding by being calm, poised, and balanced."

*"<u>Positive</u> thinking is <u>Powerful</u> thinking. If we want happiness, fulfillment, and inner peace, we must start thinking that **WE** have the power to achieve those things. Focus on the bright side of life and expect positive results."*

*"Never discredit your **Gut Instinct**. You are not paranoid. Your body can pick up on bad vibrations. If something deep inside of you, your conscious says that something is not right, trust it.*

*That's your **Gut Instinct**."*

*"**Life** is short, live it. **Love** is rare, grab it. **Anger** is always*

tasking, dump it. **Fear** *is distressing, face it.* **Memories** *are sweet, cherish them."*

"If you think you are at the 'light at the end of the tunnel,' you're not. Step back, climb up on the 'rock of life' behind you, and rediscover your next move."

Thomas J. Snee, M.Ed.

"Don't worry, there's always a light at the end of every tunnel. Hard times do not last. We may have experienced pain, sadness, confusion, and anxiety; however, we just need to have faith, and we will get through this. Often, no matter how hard life gets, it is up to us to pick up the pieces and continue. Stay positive!"

"This is my life, my story, my book. I will not let anyone else write it; nor will I apologize for the edits I make."

Steve Maraboli

"You can't change what's going on around you until you start changing what's going on within you!"

Toby Mac

"Never put the key to your happiness in somebody else's pocket."

"Don't get discouraged. A **positive attitude** *is one of the most important attributes anyone can have. Remember, everyone has bad days, but if we maintain a* **positive attitude***, we will find ways to overcome all the obstacles and challenges we encounter and face. It is up to us to live a positive and fulfilling life. Don't let circumstances and events keep us down or define who we are!"*

"Happiness is a mental attitude."

"4 Ls: Listen, Learn, Love, and Let go."

"It is amazing what you can accomplish if you do not care who gets the credit."

Harry S. Truman, 33rd President of the United States

"Leaders don't force people to follow,
they invite them on a JOURNEY."

Charles S. Lauer

<u>A</u>MBITION

"An intrinsic inner force, when featured, that springboards a proven course of positive energy, towards a desired point of reference which can only benefit everyone."

"It takes courage and strength to climb to the top."

"Body-building isn't just flexing your muscles, but rather, the expansion of your mind, talents, and hands to reach out and hold on to someone."

Thomas J. Snee, M.Ed.

"Reaching out, pulling towards you, to stand together, is EQUALITY."

Thomas J. Snee, M.Ed.

"The man who moves a mountain begins by carrying away small stones for others."

Thomas J. Snee, M.Ed.

"Pay it forward, and it will always come back."

Thomas J. Snee, M.Ed.

"On the thought of expression, that's where it comes from; it is still you. Your choice is to do with it as you may."

Joseph P. Moore

"Greed is the lack of confidence in one's own ability to be creative."

Vanna Bonta

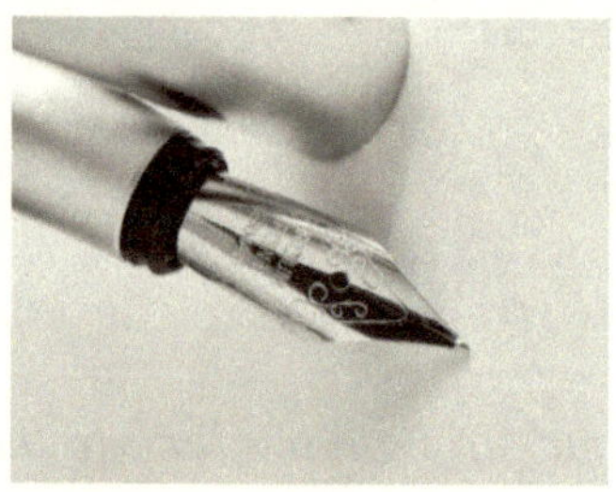

"When writing a book, it's not the words, but the thoughts that will 'fast forward' to self-dominance."

Thomas J. Snee, M.Ed.

"Tomorrow is the first blank page of a 365-page book. **Write** *a good one."*

Brad Paisley

"The triangle of success: Family, Career, and Self!"

Thomas J. Snee, M.Ed.

"Be willing to make decisions. That's the most important quality in a good leader."

George S. Patton, General, U.S. Army

"Lead by inspiration, not intimidation."

Rebecca Aguilar

"Touching any part of your body is to touch the perfection of life itself."

"Life is a gift that God gave us and that we should always put to good use, keeping it going, for all mankind."

Liam Brennan

"Life is good and precious and a moment that we must always treasure and protect."

Liam Brennan

"Compel yourself to do something you would rather not do."

"Science is not always the straight line to success."

Thomas J. Snee, M.Ed.

"We don't meet people by accident. They are meant to cross our paths for a reason!"

"Let us not become weary in always doing well. Rather, at the proper time, we will reap a profitable 'harvest' if we do not give up."

"Common sense is not a gift, it's a punishment, because you have to deal with everyone who doesn't have it."

"You were born to be real, not to be perfect."

"Ignorance *can be educated.* **Crazy** *can be medicated. But there is not a cure for being* **stupid.** *"*

"You are FREE TO **CHOOSE,** *but you are* **NOT FREE** *from the* **CONSEQUENCES** *of your* **CHOICES!"**

"Show me an enthusiastic leader, and I will show you an enthusiastic workforce. If the leader has a bad day, the whole organization has a bad day too."

"Leadership is earned, not designated."

"We are drowning in information, while starving for wisdom."

"Keep putting out good. It will come back to you tenfold, in unexpected ways."

"It is <u>always</u> your next move."

"Giving is the 'master key' to human development for all."

Thomas J. Snee, M.Ed.

"If you do not like where you are, move. You are not a tree. The world will adjust!"

"Promise me you will always remember: You are **BRAVER**

than you believe; **STRONGER** *than you seem; and* **SMARTER** *than you think."*

"The moment where you doubt whether you can fly, you cease for ever being able to do it."

– Peter Pan

"When it comes to people in your life, be a priority, not an option."

"If you remember anything about me after I leave this world, remember that **I loved** *when it was foolish and* **I cared** *when it was unwanted. When my body is gone, please remember my heart."*

"Look for something positive in each day, even if some days you have to look a little harder. Let the challenges make you stronger."

"God has a tendency of picking up a **NOBODY***, to be* **SOMEBODY***, in front of* **EVERYBODY***, without consulting* **ANYBODY***."*

"Encourage, lift, and strengthen one another. For the positive energy you spread to someone will always be felt by all."

"You never know the value of what you have until you lose it. So, cherish the people and the moments that you have in your life now."

"The 'certainty' of the 'uncertain' will create and boldly thrust us to be 'certain.' We just need to explore all the right options in the many places and times, to reconnect with those continuums of 'certainties.' Your hidden drive will spawn that spirit and articulate the absolute best of who YOU are in others to allow them to articulate and demonstrate from within their daily lives. That is the domain of 'certainty.' Do you agree? **CERTAINLY!***"* :)

Thomas J. Snee, M.Ed.

"Happiness is your responsibility. If you depend on or wait for other people to make you happy, you'll always be disappointed."

"Once upon a time, a wise man was asked, 'What is the meaning of life?' He replied, 'Life itself has no meaning. Rather, life is an opportunity to create a meaning."

"When things seem hopeless, life has a way of defying the odds, overcoming the obstacles, and coming back strong. So never give up, regardless of how hopeless things may seem. There is <u>ALWAYS</u> a way."

"Life is a journey, so jump on and enjoy the ride."

"Happiness begins with facing life with a smile and a wink!"

"People will throw stones at you. Do not throw them back. Collect them all and build an empire."

"Don't let your limitations overshadow your talents."

18 FAMOUS "WOODENISMS"

Coach John Wooden

Wooden was a philosopher without even realizing it. His perfectly succinct and simple sayings inspired many thousands of young college basketball players at UCLA and many more individuals far and wide—many of whom never stepped foot on a basketball court to hear the words straight from his mouth. That is how powerful his words were.

John Wooden's own favorite saying was "Make each day your masterpiece." But everyone has their favorite "Woodenisms," as many fans of the humble philosopher call his motivational quotes. Here are 18 of John Wooden's most famous "Woodenisms."

1. 'It's not so important who starts the game but who finishes it.'

2. 'Be more concerned with your character than your reputation, because your character is what you really are, while your reputation is merely what others think you are.'

3. 'Happiness begins where selfishness ends.'

4. 'Never lie, cheat, or steal.'

5. 'Failing to prepare is preparing to fail.'

6. 'Failure is not fatal, but failure to change might be.'

7. 'Things turn out best for the people who make the best of the way things turn out.'

8. 'If you don't have time to do it right, when will you have time to do it over?'

9.'Success comes from knowing that you did your best to become the best that you are capable of becoming.'

10. 'Talent is God-given. Be humble. Fame is man-given. Be grateful. Conceit is self-given. Be careful.'

11. 'Ability may get you to the top, but it takes character to keep you there.'

12. 'You can't let praise or criticisms get to you. It's a weakness to get caught up in either one.'

13. 'It's what you learn after you know it all that counts.'

14. 'Be quick, but don't hurry.'

15. 'Never mistake activity for achievement.'

16. 'Winning takes talent; to repeat takes character.'

17. 'Make each day your masterpiece.'

18. 'Don't let what you *cannot do* interfere with what you *can do*.'

"HOW WILL YOUR 'DASH' BE MEASURED, IN <u>YOUR</u> LIFE?"

<u>The Four Agreements</u>

"Be impeccable with your word. Do not take anything personally. Don't make assumptions. Always do your best."

Don Miguel Ruiz

<u>A WISE MAN ONCE SAID</u>

"Don't be afraid to start over again. This time, you are not starting from scratch, you are starting from experience."

<u>I have learned…</u>

I have learned...

That the best classroom in the world is at the feet of an elderly person.

I have learned...

That when you're in love, it shows.

I have learned...

That just one person saying to me, 'You've made my day!' makes my day.

I have learned...

That having a child fall asleep in your arms is one of the most peaceful feelings in the world

I have learned...

That being kind is more important than being right.

I have learned...

That you should never say no to a gift from a child.

I have lyned...

That I can always pray for someone when I do not
have the strength to help him in any other way.

I have learned...

That no matter how serious your life requires you to
be, everyone needs a friend to act goofy with.

I have learned...

That sometimes all a person needs is a hand
to hold and a heart to understand.

I have learned...

That simple walks with my father around the block on summer
nights when I was a child did wonders for me as an adult.

I have learned...

That life is like a roll of toilet paper.

The closer it gets to the end, the faster it goes.

I have learned...

That money does not buy class.

I have learned...

That it is those small daily happenings that make life so spectacular.

I have learned...

That under everyone's hard shell is someone
who wants to be appreciated and loved.

I have learned...

That to ignore the facts does not change the facts.

I have learned...

That when you plan to get even with someone,

you are only letting that person continue to hurt you.

I have learned...

That love, not time, heals all wounds.

I have learned...

That the easiest way for me to grow as a person is to
surround myself with people smarter than I am.

I have learned...

That everyone you meet deserves to be greeted with a smile.

I have **learned...**

That no one is perfect until you fall in love with them.

I have learned...

That life is tough, but I am tougher.

I have learned...

That opportunities are never lost; someone
will take the ones you miss.

I have learned...

That when you harbor bitterness, happiness will dock elsewhere.

I have learned...

That I wish I could have told my mom that I love
her one more time before she passed away.

I have learned...

That one should keep his words both soft and tender,
because tomorrow he may have to eat them.

I have learned...

That a smile is an inexpensive way to improve your looks.

I have learned...

That when your newly born grandchild holds your little
finger in his little fist, you are hooked for life.

I have learned...

That everyone wants to live on top of the mountain, but all the happiness and growth occurs while you are climbing it.

I have learned...

That the less time I have to work with, the more things I get done.

"In my life, I have lived, I have loved, I have lost, I have missed, I have hurt, I have trusted, I have made mistakes, but most of all:

I have LEARNED."

"Some people could be given an entire field of roses and only see the thorns in it. Others could be given a single weed and only see the wildflower in it. Perception is a key component to gratitude. And gratitude a key component to joy."

Amy Weatherly

"Know your circle. Make sure everybody in your boat is rowing and not drilling holes when you're not looking."

Steve Maraboli

"Your success is found in your daily routine."

"A friend is a present you give yourself."

"Don't til with windmills."

"The older I get, the more I realize I don't want to be around drama, conflict, or stress. I want a cozy home, good food, and to be surrounded by happy people."

*"One of the **happiest** moments ever is when you find the **courage** to **let go** of what you can't change."*

"There are people who plot against you, who still don't know how you survived."

"It's not about being perfect. It is about the effort. When you bring that effort every single day, that's where transformation happens. That's how change occurs."

"Lead by example; listen aggressively; communicate purposefully and with meaning; create a climate of trust; look for results, not salutes; take calculated risks; go beyond standard procedures; build up your people's confidence; generate unity; and improve everyone's quality of life as much as possible."

"Getting somewhere is important. How you get there is equally important. Do the right thing, forget petty politics, don't worry about whether you're going to upset anyone, or ruffle anyone's feathers; if it is the right thing to do, figure out a way to get past the egos and get around the bureaucratic infighting, then just do it."

"Management is about persuading people to do things they do not want to do, while leadership is about inspiring people to do things they never thought they could."

"It took me a long time to understand what it means to forgive someone. I always wondered how I could forgive someone who chooses to hurt me. After a lot of soul-searching, I realized that forgiveness is not about accepting or excusing their behavior, it's about letting it go and preventing their behavior from destroying my heart."

"A goal is a dream with a deadline."

"The <u>Pessimist</u> complains about the wind. The <u>Optimist</u> expects it to change. The <u>Leader</u> adjusts the sails."

John Maxwell

"Destroy the idea that you have to be constantly working or grinding in order to be successful. Embrace the concept that rest, recovery, reflections are essential parts of the progress towards a successful and happy life."

F-E-A-R

has two meanings!
<u>F</u>orget <u>E</u>verything <u>A</u>nd <u>R</u>un!
or
<u>F</u>ace <u>E</u>verything <u>A</u>nd <u>R</u>ise.

THE CHOICE IS YOURS.

"Never lose hope because you never know what wonderful things tomorrow will bring your way."

"Don't count the days, but rather, make the days count."

*"**Knowledge** is knowing what to say and the **Wisdom** of knowing when not to say it."*

*"If you are **not willing** to learn, no one can help you. If you are **determined** to learn, no one can stop you!"*

Distractors

"Unsolicited and negative expressions that are directed at another person who otherwise would seek a virtuous and harmonious effort of character towards a peaceful and purposeful potential; they take away from the overall leadership accomplishment from within."

"Better to remain silent and be thought a fool, than to speak and to remove all doubt."

Abraham Lincoln, 16th President of the
United States of America

"No one has the right to make you feel inferior without your permission."

Eleanor Roosevelt

"To argue with a person who has renounced the use of reason is like administering medicine to the dead."

Thomas Paine, Author, *Common Sense*

"Society has gotten to the point where everybody has a right, but nobody has or accepts responsibility."

*"Four things you can never recover: The **Stone** after it is thrown. The **Word** after it has been said. The **Occasion** after it is missed. The **Time** after it is gone."*

"Never argue with stupid people. They will drag you down to their level and then beat you with experience."

Mark Twain

"When a toxic person can no longer control you, they will try to control how others see you. This misinformation will feel unfair, but always <u>stay above it,</u> *and trust that other people will eventually see the TRUTH, just like you did!"*

"Beautiful things happen in your life when you distance yourself from all negativities, including people. Always remember, you cannot change the people around you. You can, however, change the people you choose to be around."

"Is it possible to say what you need to without being rude and hateful? Yes! If you would not want someone turning down your ideas, do not turn down theirs."

"If it does not fit in conversation, then keep it to yourself. You don't need to use offensive language or words to get your point across."

*"Some people will only love you as much as they can **use** you. Their loyalty ends when the benefits stop."*

"It's okay to dislike someone, but it is never okay to disrespect, degrade, and humiliate that person."

"Where jealousy and selfish ambitions exist, there is disorder at every foul practice."

*"**Loneliness:** When cell phones are used to text and replace the one-on-one personal contact, as well as communication with the one sitting next to you, especially family."*

"No man has a good enough memory to be a successful liar."

"It has been my experience that folks who have no vices have very few virtues."

"You cannot escape the responsibility of tomorrow by evading it today."

"No one ever notices <u>your tears, your sadness,</u> or <u>your pain</u>. But everyone notices <u>your mistakes</u>."

"Don't be disrespectful and insult others just to hold your own ground. If you do, it shows how really shaky your own position is."

"Be willing to walk alone. Many who started with you won't finish with you."

"If you are taught bitterness and anger, then you will always believe you are a victim. You will feel hurt, and the twin is entitlement. So now, you think you are owed everything, and you do not have to work for it and now, you are on a bad road to nowhere because there are people who will play into that sense of victimhood and entitlement and they still won't have a job."

Condoleezza Rice

"The moment you feel like you have to prove your worth to someone is the moment you absolutely and utterly walk away."

Alysia Harris

<u>"3 Ways to Fail…"</u>

***Complain** *about everything and everybody.*
***Blame** *others for your problems.*
***Never** *be grateful.*

"Greed is a bottomless pit which exhausts the person in an endless effort to satisfy their selfish needs without ever reaching satisfaction."

Erich Fromm

"Distance yourself from people who lie to you; disrespect you; use you; and who put you down."

"Make no mistake between my **Personality** *and my* **Attitude**. *My* **Personality** *is who I am. My* **Attitude** *depends on who you are."*

"A positive mind *finds opportunity in everything. A* **negative mind** *finds fault in everything."*

"Fake friends: Once they stop talking to you, they will start talking about you. No one follows a leader who lies."

"All truths pass through three stages:

First, *it is ridiculed.* **Second,** *it is violently opposed.* **Third,** *it is accepted as being self-evident."*

Arthur Schopenhauer

"Walk away…

From arguments that lead you to be angered.

From people who deliberately put you down.

Pleasing people who never see your worth.

From judgmental people, who do not know your struggle or what you have been up against.

Your mistakes and fears will not determine your fate.

The more you walk away from things that poison your soul, the healthier you will be."

"I forgive, but I have learned a lesson. I will not hate you, but I will not ever get close enough again for you to hurt me again. I can't let my forgiveness become my foolishness."

"The only way to win with a toxic person is not to play."

<u>Reality quotes to reflect and ponder</u>*!*

"If one day you realize I haven't talked to you in a while, it's not that I don't care, it's because you pushed me away and left me there."

"I used to think the worst thing in life was to end up **all alone***. It is not. The worst thing in life is to end up with people that make you feel all* **alone***."*

Robin Williams

"Sometimes you have to give up on people. Not because you do not care, but because they do not, and draw from your energy of caring."

Thomas J. Snee, M.Ed.

"I'm used to it. I am used to being cancelled, left out, being the second option or no option at all, forgotten about, and being ignored. I am used to getting the blame for everything with no creditable resource to 'chalk up.' It is okay. So do not feel bad if you do any of these things to me. I've learned to keep my expectations low, so none of these things will matter or infringe on my world."

<u>"I won't beg</u>

...(F)or your time and attention anymore. The more you ignore me, the more I will get used to being ignored. If you stop calling me, I will stop waiting for your calls. If you stop sending me text messages and no voice contact, I will get rid of my habit of checking my phone all day. The more you stay away from me, the more I will adapt to staying away from you. One day I will finally learn to live without you and move on."

"Nothing hurts more than being ignored, replaced, rejected, and forgotten or lied to."

"Don't let people put guilt on you for not visiting or calling them. They don't visit or call you either."

"The hardest pill I had to swallow this year was learning that no matter how good you are to someone, they can and will turn their back on you, and there's absolutely nothing you can do but suck it up and keep moving forward."

Working Women

"If you must hurt other people to feel powerful, you are an extremely weak individual."

Bobby J. Matting

"It's not about being lonely, but rather, being ignored, rejected, and forgotten."

"When someone is mean, don't listen to them. When someone is rude, walk away. When someone tries to put you down, stay firm. Don't let someone else's bad behavior destroy your inner peace."

"No response <u>is</u> a response; and <u>it is</u> a powerful one. Remember that."

"Being lonely is like a storm with no rain and crying without tears."

<u>"Avoid people who:</u>

Mess with your head. Intentionally and repeatedly do and say things that they know will upset you. Expect you to prioritize them but will refuse to prioritize you. Cannot and will not apologize sincerely. Act like the victim when they are confronted with their abusive behavior."

"You can't force people to respect you, but you can refuse to tolerate their disrespect."

"Stop expecting **LOYALTY** *from people who can't even give you* **HONESTY**.*"*

"People don't abandon people they love. People abandon people they were using."

"A negative mind will never give you a **positive life."**

"TRUST takes years to build, seconds to break, and forever to repair."

"Let me tell you this: if you meet a loner, no matter what they tell you, it's not because they enjoy solitude, it's because they have tried to blend into the world before, and people continue to disappoint them."

"Once you feel avoided by someone, never disturb them again."

"Discredited 'lip-service,' directed at someone, is the highest form of dishonor, defamation, and humiliation that can be expressed in attacking another person's character, dignity, and self-worth."

Thomas J. Snee, M.Ed.

"Never lie to someone who trusts you and never trust someone that lies to you."

"If they miss you, they will call. If they want you, they'll say it. If they care, they'll show it. And if not, they are not worth your time."

On Belittling Others

"The minute you think you have the right to belittle others because you think you're better than them, is the same minute you've proven you're worse."

Joanne Crisner Alcayaga, Writer

*"Some people will never be loyal to you; they are only loyal to **their** need of you. Once **their need** changes, so does their loyalty."*

"The moment you put a stop to people taking advantage of and disrespecting you, is when they define you as difficult, selfish, or crazy. Manipulators hate boundaries."

"Silence is better than unnecessary drama."

*"A toxic person <u>will never</u> change. They just change victims and <u>blame</u> **everything on everybody else."***

"Distance yourself from the vain."

*"You don't 'lose' friends because **REAL** friends can't be lost. You lose people masquerading as friends and you're **BETTER** for it."*

"A wise man can always be found alone. A weak man can always be found in a crowd."

"The most damaging phrase in the English language is, 'We have always done it this way'!"

RADM Grace Hopper, USN

*"I would rather adjust **my** life to your absence, than adjust **my** boundaries to accept your disrespect!"*

"A positive mind finds opportunity in everything. A negative mind finds fault in everything."

Unknown

Walk Away *from people who put you down.*

Walk Away *from fights that will never be resolved.*

Walk Away *from trying to please people who will never see your worth.*

The more you **Walk Away** *from the things that poison your soul, the healthier you will be."*

"Fear an ignorant man more than a liar."

"No response is a response. And it is a powerful one. Remember that."

Educators

"The *mentors and coaches* of the world who seek fundamental networking proficiencies to enhance the needed compatibilities and values to enrich a more fertile cultivation and nurturing harvest in the lives of future learners."

"A Navy Chief should always be a mentor, an advocate, and a receptive listener."

Thomas J. Snee, M.Ed.

"You can lead a human to knowledge, but you cannot make them think."

"The mediocre teacher tells. The good teacher explains. The superior teacher demonstrates. The great teacher inspires."

William A. Ward

"Hit me with some knowledge."

Brent Snyder

"Teachers don't teach for the 'income.' Teachers teach and inspire learning for the 'outcome'!"

"To teach is to touch a life, forever."

"Teach young people <u>how</u> to think, not <u>what</u> to think."

"Students learn because of the relationships they have with their teachers."

Steven M. Constantino, E.Edu

"A TEACHER opens minds and touches Hearts."

"A good **EDUCATION** *begins at* **HOME**. *You cannot blame a school for not nurturing values in your child that you have* <u>not</u> *instilled at home."*

"I hope one day my students can look back on the time they spent in my classroom and still feel the love I have for them, smile warmly at some of the memories, and definitely have the confidence in themselves that they can amount to everything they put their minds to."

"Every great achiever is inspired by a **great mentor.**"

Lailah Gifty Akita

"To be a **GREAT TEACHER** *you do not need the latest technology, the cutest classroom, or the newest outfit. What you do need is a passion for learning, and the heart to love every student who enters* **YOUR** *classroom."*

"Teachers need our active support and encouragement. They are doing one of the most necessary and exacting jobs in the land. They are developing our most precious national resource: our children, our future citizens."

Dwight D. Eisenhower,
34th President of the United States

"The function of education is to teach one to think intensively and to think critically. Intelligence plus character is the goal of true education."

Martin Luther King, Jr.

Men**T**or
Inspir**E**
Educ**A**te
Coa**C**h
SHare
Influ**E**ence
Encou**R**age

"Mentoring is a brain to pick, an ear to listen, and a push in the right direction!"

"The best teachers are those who show you where to look, but don't tell you what to see."

"A **COACH** *will impact more young people in a year THAN THE AVERAGE PERSON DOES IN A* **LIFETIME."**

"Be SILENT, & LISTEN. Then, go out and be a mentor and coach to LEAD, so that others may be like you!"

Thomas J. Snee, M.Ed.

"Education is not the learning of facts, but the training of the mind to think."

Albert Einstein, Scientist

"A <u>mentor</u> is someone who sees more talent and ability within you than you see in yourself, and will try to help bring it out of you!"

"Be teachable, be receptive, and always learn. You're not always right."

"If your plan is for 1 year, plant rice. If your plan is for 10 years, plant trees. If your plan is for 100 years, educate children."

Confucius

Respect

"A recognized set of behaviors from the actions of progressive thinkers, in self-composures, criterions, and critiques, that will channel to an upright character of self-worth and dignity to others."

"A man's judgment is best when he can forget about himself and his reputation, which he may have acquired, and who can concentrate wholly on making the right decisions."

ADM Raymond Spruance, USN

"It wasn't his generalship that made him stand out. It was the way he attended to and stuck by his men. His soldiers knew that he respected and cared for them, and that he would share their most severe hardships."

Edward G. Lengel, when speaking about
General George Washington

"I would rather build my character on a solid foundation of caring and supporting others, than trampling all over them in a crumbling, despairing way that will only cheapen their dignity."

Thomas J. Snee, M.Ed.

"B O S S: *Being On Spot Sincerely.*"

Thomas J. Snee, M.Ed.

*"Greed is a bottomless pit that can exhaust a person to an endless effort to satisfy **their** needs, without ever reaching for satisfaction."*

Erich Fromm

"If serving is below you, leadership is beyond you."

Anonymous

"I would rather be alone with dignity than in a relationship that requires me to sacrifice my self-respect."

"I'm not impressed by your looks, money, social status, or job title. I am impressed by the way you treat other human beings."

Vala Afshar

"A person who feels <u>appreciated</u> *will always do more than what is expected."*

"When you believe in a person, you always work harder for their cause!"

*"You are never too important to be **nice** to people."*

*"I've learned that people will forget what you said, people will forget what you did, but people will **never** forget how you made them feel welcomed."*

Maya Angelou

"It doesn't matter how old you are or where you're from. ***MANNERS, KINDNESS, RESPECT, and COMPASSION*** *will always be the sign of a decent human being."*

"If you tell the truth, you don't have to remember anything."

Mark Twain

"One of the truest signs of maturity is the ability to disagree with someone while still remaining respectful."

"*In a world where you can be anything***, <u>BE KIND!</u>"**

"A person who knows they have had enough is rich!"

"Knowledge will give you power, but character respect."

Bruce Lee

"Respect for ourselves guides our morals; respect for others guides our manner."

Laurence Sterne

"A man's character may be learned from the adjectives which he habitually uses in conversation."

Mark Twain

"Without a sense of caring, there can be no sense of community."

Anthony J. D'Angelo, Brainy Quote

"People can say they care, but it means nothing until they prove it."

*"I have learned from basic 'leadership models' and 'mentors' to live by **FIVE** words that clearly describe the excellence and character of a caring leader. Together, they set apart three 'virtues of quality, character, and of a well-poised person'. See if you agree."*

<u>I'm Sorry</u>++++++**Humility!**
<u>Thank You</u> +++++++ **Appreciation!**
<u>Please</u>+++++++++++++++++***To*** **Acknowledge!**

Thomas J. Snee, M.Ed.

"Treat people the way you want to be treated. Talk to people the way you want to be talked to. Respect is earned, not given."

<u>"Here's what's cool:"</u>

Being a mentor.
Saying 'thank you.'
Showing up on time.
Being nice to strangers.
Following your dreams.
Admitting you were wrong.
Holding doors open for others.
Listening without interrupting.
Learning and using people's names.

"Many people will walk in and out of your life, but only <u>TRUE</u> friends will leave footprints in your heart."

Eleanor Roosevelt

"Having a bad attitude is like having a flat tire. You won't get anywhere until you change it."

"When people hurt you over and over, think of them as sandpaper. They may scratch and hurt a bit, but in the end, you end up polished and they end up useless."

<u>"I was raised to show respect.</u>"

"I was taught to knock before I opened a door. Say hello when I entered a room. Say please and thank you, and to have respect for my elders. I let another person have my seat if they needed it. Say 'yes sir' and 'no sir' and help others when they needed me to, not stand on the sidelines and watch. Hold the door for the person behind me, say 'excuse me' when it's needed, and to love people for who they are and not for what I can get from them. Most importantly, I was raised to treat people exactly how I would like to be treated by others. **It's called respect."**

"Show respect to people who don't even deserve it; not as a reflection of their character, but as a reflection of yours."

Dave Willis

"RESPECT: *Listen, Learn, Lead."*

"I have read some exit surveys and conducted interviews by the military only to find out why people are leaving. I assumed that low pay would be the first reason, but in fact it was the fifth. The top reason was not being treated with respect or with dignity; second, was being prevented from making an impact on the organization; third, not being listened to; and fourth, not being rewarded with more responsibility."

"The **BEST LEADERS** *have a high consideration factor. They really care about their people."*

Brian Tracy

"If you're going to be known for something, be known for your kindness and compassion."

Dr. Shawne.com

"Whether it is FRIENDSHIP or RELATIONSHIP, all bonds are built on **TRUST.** *Without it, you have nothing."*

*"***RESPECT** *is for those who deserve it, not for those who demand it."*

"People ask me why it is so hard to trust people. The real question is, why is it so hard for people to tell the truth?"

"Sometimes in life we just need a hug...no words, not advice, just a hug to make you feel **YOU MATTER.** *"*

Soul Mends

*"***Integrity***: The choice between what's convenient and what's right."*

Tony Dungy, Football Coach

"Being a person of **INTEGRITY** *doesn't mean being* **PERFECT.** *It means being* **AUTHENTIC."**

"Our prime purpose in this life is to help others. And if you cannot help them, at least don't hurt them."

Dalai Lama

"If you can't be kind, be quiet."

"Be **impeccable** *with your words. Speak with* **integrity***. Say only what you mean. Avoid using words to speak against yourself or gossip about others and use the power of your words in the direction of* **truth, inspiration, and motivation."**

"<u>Before</u> *you assume, learn the facts.* <u>Before</u> *you judge, understand, and ask why.* <u>Before</u> *you hurt someone, 'feel.'* <u>Before</u> *you speak,* <u>THINK!</u>"

"**Speak** *in ways that others will want to listen to you.* **Listen** *in such a way that others will want to speak with you.*"

"*I am only a 'servant to the cause' and a 'minister to respect reasoning'.*"

Thomas J. Snee, M.Ed.

"*Life is not important except when it has impacted other lives.*"

"*Being an introvert is hoping to be invited but not wanting to go anywhere. Being lonely at home is not wanting anyone in your space unless you really like them. And even if you really like them, you want them to go home soon.*"

Daniel Radcliffe

"*Change begins with understanding the challenges, and also giving respect.*"

Thomas J. Snee, M.Ed.

"*I'm old-school. I believe in having good manners, respecting my elders, and helping others when I can.*"

"*Don't sacrifice your peace of mind trying to point out someone's true colors. Lack of character always reveals itself in the end.*"

"If your absence brings me peace, I didn't lose you."

Steve Maraboli

"In order to empathize with someone's experience, you should be willing to believe them as they see it and not how you imagine their experience to be."

Brene Brown

*"**TRUTH** does not mind being questioned.*

*A **LIE** does not like being challenged."*

"No matter how educated, talented, rich, or cool you believe you are, how you treat people ultimately tells all.

INTEGRITY is EVERYTHING."

S̲ELF-CHARACTER & CONFIDENCE

"The authenticity of one's heart, soul, conscience, and spirit that contributes to a solid turf of valor, driven to a profound cause."

"The stepping out and bridging is the 'hand-to-hand' stronghold towards any success."

Thomas J. Snee, M.Ed.

"Never point a finger at someone. Rather, hold out your hand, take a firm grip, smile, pull, and move forward together."

Thomas J. Snee, M.Ed.

THINGS to Remember!

"The two most important days in your life are the day you are born and the day you found out why."

Mark Twain

"I am not a product of my circumstances. I am a product of my decisions."

Stephen Covey

"Tell me and I will forget. Teach me and I will remember. Involve me and I will learn."

Benjamin Franklin, Statesman

"The world is changed by your example, not by your opinion."

Paulo Coelho

*"Be more concerned with your character than your reputation. Your character is what you really are, while your reputation is merely what others think of **who** you are."*

John Wooden

"Only a man's character is the real criterion of worth."

Eleanor Roosevelt, First Lady

"I just need you around. Don't question the methods."

Joseph P. Moore

"Leadership is not a position, but an opportunity to serve the most vulnerable".

Thomas J. Snee, M.Ed.

"When your heart is pure, your mind is clear!"

*"Disciplining yourself to do what you know is **right and important,** although difficult, is the **highroad to pride,** self-esteem, and personal satisfaction."*

Margaret Thatcher, Prime Minister, Great Britain

"It's okay, not to be okay. People struggle all the time, for all sorts of reasons. For some it is a permanent condition, for others it can be temporary. But whatever their situation is, the way they feel is normal."

"A positive attitude will always cause a chain reaction of affirmative thoughts, events, and outcomes. It is the catalyst, the spark, and that will invigorate extraordinary results."

"In life, it's important to know when to stop arguing with people and simply let them be wrong."

"The foundation stones for a balanced, successful person are honesty, character, integrity, faith, love, and loyalty."

Zig Ziglar

"Doom and gloom does not motivate; it desecrates the very human spirit to move on!"

"It's okay for you to believe what you believe. It is not okay, however, for you to insist that everyone else believe the same as you."

"Since you get more joy out of giving joy to others, you should put a good deal of thought into the happiness that you are able to give."

Eleanor Roosevelt, First Lady

"The way to get started is to quit talking and begin doing."

Walt Disney

"No matter what happens in life, be good to people. Being good to people is a wonderful legacy to leave behind."

"Your **SMILE** *is your* **LOGO,** *your PERSONALITY is your BUSINESS CARD, how you leave others feeling after an experience with you becomes your* **TRADEMARK."**

Jay Danzie

"Character is how you treat those who can do nothing for you."

"I follow three rules: Do the right thing, do the best you can, and always show people you care."

Lou Holtz, Football Coach, Notre Dame University

"Don't destroy or tear down another person's self-confidence or dignity. They are a success by who they are and thus, should be given that 'back-bone' to enjoy that success."

Thomas J. Snee, M.Ed.

"Believe in yourself and you will succeed."

"A person who will not stand for principles will fall for anything."

WATCH YOUR…

"THOUGHTS; *they lead to attitudes.*
ATTITUDES; *they lead to words.*
WORDS; *they lead to actions.*
ACTIONS; *they lead to habits.*
HABITS; *they form your character.*
CHARACTER; *it determines your destiny."*

"<u>COMPROMISING</u> *doesn't mean that you are wrong*

& someone is right. It only means that **YOU value your 'RELATIONSHIP'** *MUCH MORE THAN YOUR 'EGO' "*

Vacks Quotes

"Compromise is not about losing. It is about deciding that the other person has just as much right to be happy with the result as you do."

"When you cannot control what is happening, challenge yourself to control the way you respond to what's happening. That's where your power is."

"Be strong enough to stand alone, smart enough to know when you need help, and brave enough to ask for it."

Pb

"To make a difference in someone's life, you do not have to be brilliant, rich, beautiful, or perfect. You just have to care."

Mandy Hale

"I have come to the realization that I have sacrificed too much of my own mental health and self-care for the benefit of everybody else's. It is time to step back, re-evaluate, and take care of myself. I'm happy that I have the support of my loved ones in this journey."

"Strength grows in the moments when you think you can't go on, but you keep going anyway."

"*Compassion and tolerance are not signs of weakness, but of strength."*

Dalai Lama

"Integrity is the essence of everything successful."

"Believe in yourself, and you will succeed, because very few people will."

"Character is what you are in the dark."

"Your abilities may get you to the top, but only your character will keep you there."

"To give without any reward, or any notice, has a special quality of its own."

Anne Morrow Lindbergh

"Your many hidden talents will become obvious to those around you."

"Human beings grow best with encouragement and love. Today, let every word you speak (to yourself and others) be filled with **KINDNESS!"**

"Always remember to fall asleep with a dream and wake up with a purpose."

"Getting somewhere is important. How you get there is equally important. Do the right thing, forget the petty politics, don't worry about whether you're going to upset anyone, or ruffle anyone's feathers; if it is the right thing to do, figure out a way to get past the egos and a way to get around the bureaucratic infighting, and then just do it."

"Trust is earned when actions meet words."

Chris Butler

"TRUST *starts with the* **TRUTH** *and ends with the* **TRUTH**. *"*

"Trust doesn't come with a refill. Once it is gone, you probably will not get it back, and if you do, it will never be the same! <u>THAT'S A FACT!"</u>

"Do the right thing, even when no one is looking. It's called **integrity."**

"Remember, in **'DEPRESSION'***, you can always say,* **'I PRESSED ON.'** *Same letters, only to move on!"*

"Knowing when to walk away is **Wisdom**. *Being able to walk away is* **Courage**. *Walking away with your head held high is* **Dignity***."*

"Never think that what you have to offer is insignificant. There will always be someone out there who needs what you have to give."

"For where there is jealousy and selfish ambitions, there is disorder of every kind of foul practice."

James: 3:16

"Without self-discipline, success is impossible, **PERIOD."**

"Maturity comes when you stop making excuses and start making changes."

<u>Acceptance</u> *does not mean resignation.*

It means, *Understanding that something is what it is and there has got to be a way* **THROUGH** *it."*

Michael J. Fox

"Acceptance *is the harshest lesson life teaches and the one most important to learn."*

"The first step toward change is awareness. The second step is acceptance."

Nathaniel Branden

"The Stronger you become, the gentler you will be."

"The three <u>C</u>s in life are: <u>C</u>hoices, <u>C</u>hances, and <u>C</u>hanges – **YOU,** *make a <u>C</u>hoice, to take a <u>C</u>hance, or your life will never <u>C</u>hange."*

"One of the best lessons you can learn to master is how to remain calm."

~~Note to Self~~

""What is my purpose in Life?' I asked.

'What if I told you that you fulfilled it when you took an extra hour to talk to that kid about his life?' said the voice.

'Or when you paid for that young couple in the restaurant? Or when you saved that dog in traffic? Or when you tied your father's shoes for him?

Your problem is that you equate your purpose with goal-based achievements. The universe is not interested in your achievements, just your heart. When you choose to act out of kindness, compassion, and love, you are already aligned with your true purpose. No need to look any further!'"

"Your past successes will only be overshadowed by your future successes."

"Gratitude is the memory of the heart."

Jean Baptiste Massieue

"Never blame anyone in your life. The good people give you happiness. The bad people give you experience. The worst people give you a lesson. The best people give you memories."

"To make a difference in someone's life, you do not have to be brilliant, rich, beautiful, or perfect. You just have to care."

"No act of kindness, no matter how small, is ever wasted."

Aesop

"We cannot change anything unless we accept it."

Carl Jung

*"**FREEDOM** flourishes upon the bedrock of ethics and integrity."*

Mollie Marti

"True wisdom comes to each of us when we realize how little we understand about life, ourselves, and the world around us."

"Learn to be okay with people not knowing your side of the story. You have nothing to prove to anyone."

"Nothing can stop a person with the right mental attitude from

achieving their goal, and nothing on earth can help that person with a wrong mental attitude."

"Leadership is not a position or title in life. Rather, it is actions and examples you show, model, and demonstrate to others."

"Never ignore a person who cares for you. Someday you will realize you have lost a diamond while you were collecting stones."

*"**A strong friendship** doesn't need daily conversation, approval, or being together. If the friendship lives in the heart, true friends never part."*

"A hunch is creativity trying to tell you something."

"Happiness can exist only in acceptance."

"True friends are those who lift you up when no one else even noticed you were down."

"We may not choose our circumstances, but we do get to choose our attitude and response."

Toby Mac, #SPEAKLIFE

"WINNERS are not people who never fail, but people who never quit."

"Have a healthy relationship with others. Not just in goals, nor money, achievements, or titles, just a healthy relationship with others."

Thomas J. Snee, M.Ed.

THE IMPORTANT THINGS IN LIFE!

"A Master Chief stood before his audience at a Chief conference with some items on the table in front of him.

When the lecture began, without a word, the Master Chief picked up a large and empty mayonnaise jar and proceeded to fill it with rocks, about two inches in diameter. The Master Chief then asked the audience if the jar was full. They agreed that it was.

So, the Master Chief then picked up a box of pebbles and poured them into the jar. He shook the jar lightly. The pebbles, of course, rolled into the open areas between the rocks. The Master Chief then asked the audience again if the jar was full. They agreed it was.

The Master Chief picked up a box of sand and poured it into the jar. Of course, the sand filled up the remaining open areas of the jar. The Master Chief then asked once more if the jar was full. The audience responded with a unanimous "Yes."

"Now," said the Master Chief, "I want you to recognize that this jar represents your life. The rocks are the important things – your family, your partner, your health, and your children – things that if everything else was lost and only they remained, your life would still be full."

"The pebbles are the other things that matter – like your job, your house, your car. The sand is everything else, the small stuff. If you put the sand into the jar first," the Master Chief continued, "there is no room for the pebbles or the rocks. The same goes for your life. If you spend all your time and energy on the small stuff, you will never have room for the things that are important to you."

Pay attention to the things that are critical to your happiness. Play with your children. Take your partner out dancing. There will always be time to go to work, clean the house, or fix the disposal.

"Take care of the rocks first – the things that really matter. Set your priorities. The rest is just sand."

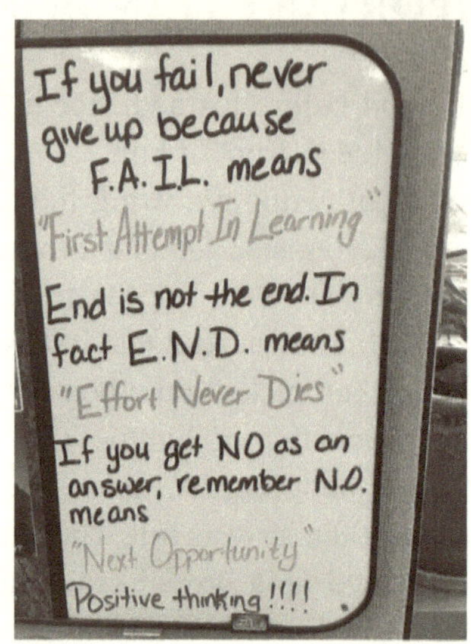

*"Sometimes you **win,** sometimes you **learn**."*

*"**Experience** tells you* what to do; **confidence** *allows you* to do it."

"Your value doesn't decrease based on someone's inability to see your warmth."

"Strong people stand up for themselves, but STRONGER people stand up for others."

*"We can't control everything that happens to us, but we <u>CAN</u> control the way we respond. Most of our stresses come directly from the way we think and respond to different things. If we adjust our **attitude**, all the extras will disappear."*

"People will throw stones at you. Do not throw them back. Collect them all and build an empire."

"Always help someone. You might be the only one that does."

"The ultimate test of your greatness is the way you treat every human being."

Pope St. John Paul II

"Everyone you meet is fighting a battle you know nothing about. Be kind, ALWAYS."

"You can preach a better sermon with your life than with your lips."

"A man's character may be learned from the adjectives which he habitually uses in conversation."

Mark Twain

Six Ethics of Life

Before you Pray – **Believe.**
Before you Speak – **Listen.**
Before you Spend – **Earn.**
Before you Write – **Think.**
Before you Quit – **Try &**
Before you Die – **Live!**

"Your heart will always make itself known through your words."

"Never ruin an apology with an excuse."

Benjamin Franklin

"Look for three things in a person: **Intelligence, Energy, and Integrity**. *If they do not have the last one, do not even bother with the first two."*

Warren Buffet

"A heart without character in honesty, content, or conduct will never manifest itself towards progress."

Thomas J. Snee, M.Ed.

"Integrity is the essence of everything successful."

"Maturity is when you have the power to destroy someone who did you wrong, but instead you just breathe, walk away, and let life take care of them."

"Optimism is the fundamental foundation of all, and the most important of all human traits. It allows us to evolve our attitudes, to improve our situations, and to hope for a better tomorrow, no matter what is going on around us today. We must never stop believing!"

"Depression is not a sign of weakness; it is a sign that you have been strong for too long."

"Kindness reveals all justice, while wisdom defines it."

Thomas J. Snee, M.Ed.

"You must be big enough to admit your mistakes, smart enough to learn from them, and strong enough to correct them."

John C. Maxwell

"A Hero Is...

One who never hesitates to tackle the most difficult of problems.

One who is always by your side! One who knows right from wrong!

One who acts with pride! A Hero touches every one of us, whether it is in word or deed, and isalways tending to those who find themselves in need. When a Hero leaves this earth, yes, it is sad, but true, all too many times... That Hero is dressed in blue."

"Some people think that to be strong is to never feel pain. In reality, the strongest people are the ones who feel it, understand it, and accept it."

"When someone tries to trigger you by insulting you or by doing or saying something that irritates you, take a deep breath and switch off your ego. Remember that if you are easily offended, you are easily manipulated."

"Being honest might not get you a lot of friends, but it will always get you the right ones."

John Lennon

"It is when I struggle that I am strengthened. It is when I am challenged to my core, that I learn from the depths of who I am."

Steve Maraboli

"You gotta understand the difference between someone who speaks to you on their free time and someone who frees their time to speak to you."

"Don't judge my choices when you don't understand my reasons."

"When you show up authentic, you create the space for others to do the same. WALK IN YOUR TRUTH."

"Character is how you live your life when no one is looking around. Be you, the person you are as a 'real person.' This will allow you to stand out to others."

Thomas J. Snee, M.Ed.

"People who have bad attitudes often blame their disposition on others or on various circumstances, but the fact is that each of us is responsible for our own attitude."

Tony Cooke

*"Leadership through character defined is:
be curious, be creative, be caring, and be confident."*

Thomas J. Snee, M.Ed.

"The longer I live, the more I realize that **real strength** *has much more to do with what is* **not seen. Real strength** *has to do with* **helping others."**

Mr. Fred Rogers

"The supreme quality for leadership is unquestionable integrity. Without it, no real success is possible."

Dwight D. Eisenhower, 34th President of
the United States of America

"I would rather build my character on a solid foundation of caring and supporting others, than trampling all over them in a crumbling despairing way that will only cheapen their dignity."

Thomas J. Snee, M.Ed.

"The **BEST LEADERS** *have a high consideration factor. They really care about and respect their people."*

Brian Tracy

"Surround yourself with people who talk about their visions, ideas, dreams, and faith; not those who talk about other people."

Charles F. Glassman

"If money and material things make you believe that you are better than others, you are the poorest person on earth."

Women Working

Humility

"The *'mirror of life'* when reflecting sincere responsibility and tranquility through the efforts affecting another's judgement in their actions."

"Humility is serving all peoples."

"Don't be impressed by: Money, Titles, Degrees, or Looks. Be impressed by: Generosity, Integrity, Humility, and Kindness."

Vala Afshar

"I hope I shall have possessed the firmness and virtue enough to maintain what I consider the most enviable of all titles, the character of an Honest Man."

George Washington, 1st President of
the United States of America

*"Don't ever mistake my silence for **ignorance,** my calmness for **acceptance,** and my kindness for **weakness.**"*

"Character is like a tree and your reputation is like its shadow. The shadow is what we think of it; the tree is the real thing."

Abraham Lincoln, 16th President of the United States

"True humility is not thinking less of yourself; it is thinking of yourself less."

C. S. Lewis

"The moment you feel like you have to prove your worth to someone, is the moment you absolutely need to walk away."

"Sometimes we just need to give 'hand-to-hand' forgiveness."

"I'm not interested in whether you've stood with the great. I'm interested in whether you've sat with the broken."

"If you have to choose between being kind and being right, choose being kind and you will always be right."

"The sensitivity that you show and share towards others will always come back to you."

"Life is not being rich, being popular, being highly educated, or being perfect. It is about being real, being humble, and being kind."

"You're never too important to be nice to people."

"A fouled anchor is a symbol of humility."

"I'm beginning to see and experience that a 'Lifetime Achievement Award' is nothing more than tolerance with a purpose."

Thomas J. Snee, M.Ed.

"No person was ever honored for what he received. Honor has been the reward for what he gave."

Calvin Coolidge, 30th President of the United States

"Sometimes the strongest among us are the ones who smile through silent pain, cry behind closed doors, and fight battles nobody knows about."

Dave's Words of Wisdom

"Never once did I ever do anything to promote myself, just the organization."

"Being humble means recognizing **WE** *are not on earth to see how important* **WE** *can become, but to see how much difference* **WE** *can make in the lives of others."*

"He who expects no gratitude shall never be disappointed."

"Be **humble**, *take* **courage**, *show* **compassion.***"*

Thomas J. Snee, M.Ed.

"Be an encourager. The world has plenty of critics already."

"Your beliefs don't make you a better person. Your behavior does."

"Being humble means to recognize that we are not on this earth to see how important we can become, but rather, how much of a difference we can make in the lives of others."

"ALSO HIGHLY CONTAGIOUS IS – kindness, patience, love, enthusiasm, and a positive attitude.

Don't wait to catch it from others>>Be the carrier!"

"A gentleman is defined by what **he stands for**, *not by what* **he stands against**. *"*

Being Calaballero

"A mistake that **makes you humble** *is better than an achievement that makes you arrogant."*

"Life is not being rich, being popular, being highly educated, or being perfect. It is about being **HUMBLE** *and being kind."*

"It only takes a few seconds to hurt someone. But sometimes it takes years to repair the damage. Cherish the hearts that love you."

"When you screw up and you know it, just apologize. Allow yourself to be human at that moment. Do not make excuses. For me, it's not the mistake you make, it's whether or not you're willing to take responsibility for it."

Steve Maraboli

"Being HUMBLE means recognizing we are not on earth to see how important we can become, but to see HOW MUCH DIFFERENCE WE CAN MAKE in the lives of others."

Gordon B. Hinckley

"Excellence does not show up if humility is not invoked.

If humility does not exist within oneself, then arrogance creeps in and is fronted by, 'I've got this...'"

"Diligence is being the Renaissance man through trust, giving counsel, with intelligence, while being humble and always being courteous."

Thomas J. Snee, M.Ed.

"Humility and simplicity make you great."

"A fool has Certainty. A wise man has Humility."

"You never look good trying to make someone else look bad."

*"A mistake which makes you **humble** is much better than an achievement that makes you **arrogant.**"*

Inspiration

"The captivations of entrusted admirations when observed by others that autonomously become the behaviors in others."

"A hero need not speak of wisdom. When he is gone, the world will speak for him."

Joseph P. Moore

"Service to others is the rent you pay for your room here on earth."

Mohammed Ali

"Leadership is not a journey to rise in the ranks. Leadership is an opportunity to take the journey and help those around you rise."

"Our primary want should be <u>someone who will inspire us</u> to be who we know we are and can be."

Ralph Waldo Emerson

"A great person attracts great people and knows how to hold them together."

Johann Wolfgang Von Goethe

"When you demonstrate leadership, the evidence is the quality

of your actions, known for the type of <u>leader that will emerge out of your direction and leadership style.</u> *"*

Sujit Lalwani

"Real leadership is leaders that recognize that they serve the people they lead."

Pete Hoekstra, United States Ambassador to the Netherlands

"From destroyers, a cruiser, an aircraft carrier; Vietnam & Libya; serving as an Instructor, Recruiter, Career Counselor, Senior Enlisted Advisor; Classroom Middle School Teacher/ Administrator, to Capitol Hill, it all adds to just trying to make a difference for those I love, serve, and respect."

Thomas J. Snee, M.Ed.

"Never give up on someone with mental illness. When the <u>I</u> *is replaced by* <u>We</u>, <u>I</u>*llness becomes a* <u>We</u>*llness."*

Shannon L. Alder

"A seasoned master from the past always engages in mentoring others into the future."

Thomas J. Snee, M.Ed.

"It doesn't matter how old you are or where you're from, ***MANNERS, KINDNESS, RESPECT, and COMPASSION,*** *will always be the sign of a decent human being."*

"Love isn't what you say. Love is what you do!"

"Not for ourselves, but for others!"

"Non sibi sed aliis!"

"Service to others is humility."

"Servetus, ut alii, verum humilitatem!"

"Neither to oppress, nor to be oppressed, but to serve."

"Neque calumniam nec sustinebat sed ministrare."

"Common sense is instinct, and enough of it is genius."

"In case you need this today:
You are not a waste of space.
You are needed and wanted.
You are not a failure.
I believe in you.
You are loved.
You got this.
GOD LOVES YOU!"

"Don't walk behind me; I may not lead. o not walk in front of me; I may not follow. Just walk beside me and be my friend."

"Wisdom inspires understanding through fortitude and perseverance."

"Don't ever forget that just maybe **YOU** *are the Lighthouse in someone's storm."*

"Try to be a rainbow in someone else's cloud."

Maya Angelou

"So many people are hanging by the thinnest of threads. Treat people well, you could just be that thread."

"The delicate balance of mentoring someone is not creating

them in your own image but giving them the opportunity to create themselves."

Steven Spielberg

"The key to being a good mentor **is to help people become more of who they already are** *–not to make them like you."*

Suze Orman

"When you see something beautiful in someone, tell them. It may take a second to say, but for them, it could last a lifetime."

"Don't waste words on people who deserve your silence. Sometimes the most powerful thing you can say is nothing at all."

"What <u>is</u> *essential* <u>is to be</u> *respected, trusted, and effective."*

"The difference between stupidity and genius is that genius has its limits."

Albert Einstein, Scientist

"The most beautiful things in life aren't just things. They are the people, places, memories, moments, smiles, and the laughs."

"Listen & Silent *are spelled with the same letters. Think about it."*

"True friends are those rare people who come to find you in dark places and lead you back to the light."

Steven Aitchison

"A hero is someone who is concerned about other people's well-being and will go out of his or her way to help them, even if there is no chance of a reward."

Stan Lee

"Be the person who breaks the cycle. If you were judged, choose understanding. If you were rejected, choose acceptance. If you were shamed, choose compassion. Be the person you needed when you were hurting, not the person who hurts. Vow to be better than what broke you – to heal instead of becoming bitter so you can act from your heart, not your pain."

Lori Deschene

"Gratitude is an attitude! Share it."

Thomas J. Snee, M.Ed.

"Knowledge knows what to say. Wisdom knows whether or not to say it."

"A smart person knows what to say. A wise person knows whether or not to say it."

"Fear is excitement in need of an attitude adjustment."

"Your smile is your greatest social asset!"

Zig Zigler

"Every person from your past lives as a shadow in our minds. Good or bad, they all helped you write the story of your life, and shaped the person you are today."

"Don't give up before the miracle happens!"

"Be the change that you want to see in the world."

Ghandi

"To make a difference in someone's life, you do not have to be brilliant, rich, beautiful, or perfect. You just have to care."

*"Before having total **loyalty**, one must have total **honesty** of **mind, self, and spirit** to themselves and others.**"**

Thomas J. Snee, M.Ed.

T.H.I.N.K.

Be, <u>T</u>*ruthful,* <u>H</u>*elpful!* <u>I</u>*nspiring!* <u>N</u>*ecessary! &* <u>K</u>*ind!*

"If you see someone falling behind, walk beside them.

If you see someone being ignored, find a way to include them.

Always remind people of their worth. *One small act could mean the world to them."*

"Every **Stone** *has a story. Every* **Story** *has a meaning. Every* **Meaning** *needs dialogue. Every* **Dialogue** *is a dream. Every* **Dream** *should be grounded in* **HOPE***!"*

Thomas J. Snee, M.Ed.

"You can't go back and change the beginning, but you can start where you are and change the ending."

C.S. Lewis

"Betrayal shatters illusions. It breaks your heart but clears your vision."

Steve Maraboli

"Be the most decisive person you know. Leaders should have wills, not wishes. Being decisive, being focused, and committing ourselves to the fulfillment of a dream significantly increases our probability of success while closing the door to the wrong options."

John Mason

"Knowledge and Understanding one another in fellowship are the seeds to Progress and Wisdom."

Thomas J. Snee, M.Ed.

"Life is a tapestry by the world's greatest designer, YOU, and the needlepoint of one's character."

Thomas J. Snee, M.Ed.

Potential

"That *'One Moment in Time'* when ideas are pursued, actively demonstrated, proven, and achieved, in the destinies of future promises."

"The difference between a successful person and others is not a lack of strength, nor a lack of knowledge, but rather, a lack of will."

Vince Lombardi, NFL Football Coach, Green Bay Packers

"The ultimate measure of a man is not where he stands in moments of comfort, but where he stands in and at times of challenge and controversy."

Martin Luther King, Jr., Civil Rights Leader

"Rely on your own strengths in body and soul. Take your 'star' of self-reliance, faith, honesty, and industry. Do not take too much advice; stay at the helm of your life and steer your own ship, to the mark your intent to sail. Energy, and invincible determination with the right motivation, is the lever that will move the world."

Noah Porter

"Always, always, the plight of man is to be expressed."

Thomas J. Snee, M.Ed.

"The key to successful leadership today is influence, not authority."

Kenneth Blanchard

"A hunch is creativity trying to tell you something."

"An untapped mind is like a pearl at the bottom of the ocean begging to be noticed!"

Thomas J. Snee, M.Ed.

"Life is like a gold nugget. It is pure and valuable. When mixed with rocks, it becomes of less value. Gold, with some rocks, still has value, even if it isn't in the best of life, there is still life."

Liam Brennan

"They told me I could be whatever I wanted to be. So, I became a United States sailor!"

"Positive thinking is more than just a tagline. It changes the way we behave. You should always passionately believe that when you are positive, it not only makes you better, but also those around you."

"Always choose inclusiveness."

Thomas J. Snee, M.Ed.

"Always try to channel your <u>passions</u> and your <u>future</u> towards **sustainability**.*"*

Thomas J. Snee, M.Ed.

"We need to build communities of people!"

Thomas J. Snee, M.Ed.

"The majority of people will quit, and that's where they will stay, with the majority. Successful people want to be part of the minority, who will never quit."

"To **change** *anything, we need* **to** *know how to move* **FORWARD***; be* **CREATIVE, ADAPTIVE, RESPECTFULL, and to EMBRACE** *change. We don't always have to agree with one another, but it is always important that we appreciate and respect each other's influence in the dignity of how to make* **CHANGE!"**

Thomas J. Snee, M.Ed.

"Don't confuse recklessness with confidence."

"Here's a simple key to success in any area of your life. Be known as a person of persistence, endurance, commitment and a person who will be the one who will accomplish more than a thousand people will have done alone."

"Create bigger 'bow waves' into the future. It will always yield a better understanding from its 'wake'!"

Thomas J. Snee, M.Ed.

"Life's tragedy is when we get **OLD** *too soon and* **WISE** *too late."*

Benjamin Franklin

"The purpose of human life is to serve, and to show compassion and the will to help others."

Albert Schweitzer

"Commit yourself to those you are leading, because the moment you take the command, you become responsible for them and their success."

MCPOCG (#10) Skip Bowen, U.S. Coast Guard

<u>Risk takers...</u>

"People should get scared. It is good for our systems. Fear makes you see better, and it makes you think better--once you're used to harnessing it."

Laird Hamilton, Legendary Surfer

"If you rearrange the letters in **DEPRESSION,** *you'll get* **I PRESSED ON!** *Meaning, your current situation is* **NOT** *your destination!"*

"It's not what you go through that defines you; you can't help that. It's what you do **AFTER** *you've gone through it that really tests who you are."*

Kwame Floyd

"The **STRONGEST** *people make time to help others, even if they're struggling with their own* **personal demons."**

"Success is not final; failure is not fatal. It is the courage to continue that counts."

Winston Churchill

"I no longer listen to what people say. I just watch what they do. Behavior never lies."

Winston Churchill

"Knowledge comes from learning. Wisdom comes from living."

Quotes4sharing.com

"Knowledge is not power. Applying what you learned is."

"In my life, I have Lived, I have Loved, I have Lost, I have Missed, I have Hurt, I have Trusted, I have made Mistakes, but most of all:

I have LEARNED."

"Don't let today's disappointment cast a shadow on tomorrow's dream."

"Gossip dies when it hits a wise person's ears."

"You don't always need a plan. Sometimes you just need to breathe. **TRUST, LET GO,** *see what happens."*

"You don't always need a plan. Sometimes, you just need to breathe, trust, let go, and see what happens."

"Patience is not the ability to wait but how you act while you're waiting."

Joyce Meyer

"Your life's story could be the key that unlocks someone else's prison. Don't be afraid to share it."

"Our true scars don't heal. That is why they are scars. But each one we have makes us more of who we are. The point of a scar is not to look back on it and see what we regret, but to see what we've overcome."

"Always remember to fall asleep with a dream and wake up with a purpose."

"Sometimes the best thing you can do is not think, not wonder, not imagine, nor be obsessed. Just breathe and have faith that everything will work out for the best."

"The meaning of life is to find your gift. The purpose of life is to give it away."

Pablo Picasso

"Stop being ashamed of how many times you've fallen and start being proud of how many times you've gotten up."

"Run when you can, walk if you have to, crawl if you must; just never give up."

"Patience is not the <u>ability</u> to wait, but the <u>ability</u> to keep a good <u>attitude</u> while waiting."

"Every struggle in your life has shaped you into the person you are today. Be thankful for the hard times; they only made you stronger than you were."

"The Fantail of a Navy ship was my 'search and rescue' at the end of every day. Whenever a sailor came up and asked, 'Master Chief, do you have a minute?' I would always say, 'Sure, what's on your mind?' Never rushed, I always took time, it was never too late, and together we shared the moment!"

FORCM (SW) Thomas J. Snee, USN, (Ret), M.Ed.

"Through every dark night, there's a bright day that follows. So, no matter how hard it gets, stick your chest out, keep your head up, and handle whatever life throws at you! Always remember...what is going on today, won't last forever!"

**"BE BRAVE, BE BOLD, BE CONSIDERATE,
BE HUMBLE, BE STRONG, BE YOU!"**

"You were given this life because you are strong enough to live it."

"The aim of argument, or of a discussion, should not be victory, but progress."

Joseph Joubert

"When the debate is lost, slander becomes the tool of the losers."

Socrates

"You either get <u>bitter</u> or you get <u>better</u>. It is that simple. You either take what has been dealt to you or allow it to make you a <u>better</u> person, or you allow it to tear you down. <u>The Choice</u> does not belong to fate; it <u>belongs to you.</u>"

Josh Shipp

"Learn to be your own best friend because there are going to be days where no one is going to be there for you but yourself."

"Don't be a Prisoner of your Past! Instead, be a Pioneer of your Future."

"Giving is the 'master key', to success, in all applications of Human Life."

Bryant McGill

Eagles…

Lesson 1. "Eagles fly alone and at higher altitudes!" Stay away from narrow-minded people, and those that bring you down. Always keep good company.

Lesson 2. "Eagles look beyond and far!" Always have a vision and remain focused regardless of the obstacles; you will succeed.

Lesson 3. "Eagles don't eat dead things; they feed only on fresh prey!" Do not rely on your past accomplishments, but rather, keep searching ahead, and be a visionary for new frontiers to conquer.

Lesson 4. "Eagles love storms!" Achievers are not afraid of challenges or risks; rather, they relish them and use them profitably.

Lesson 5. "When a female Eagle meets a male Eagle, she tests him for commitment!" Whether it is your personal or professional life, always test the commitment of people intended for partnership.

Lesson 6. "Eagles prepare for training!" Leave your comfort zone; there is no growth there.

Lesson 7. "When an Eagle grows old, they hurt themselves for new feathers!" We occasionally need to shed off the old habits, pride, and things that burden us that add no value to our lives, and we need to *let it go.*

"How to become a MANGER:
"Be Empty! Be Sturdy! Be Soft inside! Be Still!
Be Ready!"

"Being a loner has a power that very few people can handle. It is not about being lonely, but rather about being ignored or forgotten. Don't jump, don't walk back, make your own LIFE."

"Being alone has a power that very few people can handle."

"The one who follows the crowd will usually go no further than the crowd. The one who walks alone is likely to find himself in places no one has ever been before."

Albert Einstein

"Hope is important because it can make the present moment less difficult to bear. If we believe that tomorrow will be better, we can deal with whatever life throws at us today. Also remember...to find happiness, we need to quit focusing on what's wrong and start focusing on what's right."

"Never underestimate the difference you can make in the lives of others. Step forward, reach out, and help. Today is that day to reach out to someone who just might need a lift or a kind word of encouragement. During these times, be the beacon of light."

"Social distancing should not be ignoring, isolating, or rejecting others, but rather, a way of <u>reaching out to touch someone's inner feelings!</u>"

Thomas J. Snee, M.Ed.

"No matter what people tell you, words and ideas can change the world."

Robin Williams

"Every person comes with a WARNING. What does yours say?

They told me I could not. That's why I did."

"If there is no struggle, there is no progress."

Frederick Douglass

Motto in Life: "You can never cross the ocean until you have the courage to lose sight of the coast."

"When you know yourself, you are empowered. When you accept yourself, you are invincible."

"We have seen many storms in our lifetime. Most storms have caught us by surprise, so that we can learn to look beyond the storm and try to understand that we are not humanly capable of controlling the weather. We need to exercise the art of being patient and to respect the fury of nature. Starting today, forget what's wrong and start appreciating what remains and look forward to what is coming next. Stars can't shine without darkness."

"Your attributes, not your aptitude, will determine your true self in attitude."

Thomas J. Snee, M.Ed.

"Reflections in Life are in the Hearts, Minds, and Souls of every person! Go out and be that person who will Lead and Shine for others to show who you really are. Listen, Love, Mentor, Coach, Let Go, but always Lead to Success!"

Thomas J. Snee, M.Ed.

WHAT IS A 'SHIPMATE'?

FORCM (SW) THOMAS J. SNEE, USN, (RET)

This question has often been expressed and shared with me. The *'white hat'*, as we were so often called, *'halfcocked'* on the back of our heads, defined us as persons, who were always searching and looking out to sea for a new life. The right foot on the lines, not to jump or surrender, but a *'leg up'* on life's challenges in thought and ideas by persons we call, *SHIPMATES!*

You see, most of us *'signed on as young men',* for the seas and a new adventure. We left our hometowns to create, make, and hopefully aim our *'shot line',* into new friendships and ports of call. No, we did not forget our hometown friends, but rather, rediscovered a whole new world. Some may think, that when our *'brows'* were pulled up, we departed, but to move on, from those *anchored* pasts. These valued bonds were left *for other gangplanks* in another life. We moved on to make new and *bigger bow waves for smoother wakes, in life's high seas.* We did not sign on to organizations or associations to be forgotten, but as persons of dignity, value, and self-worth, or simply, as *SHIPMATES.*

So, when you meet that casual friend, remember, they too are persons on a *sea detail* away from home. They were searching for a bonding as *SHIPMATES* for a new life. Sometimes lonely, but always, just a bonding in friendship, from the many *sea tales* of the past, as a *SHIPMATE.* We are not just another name on the rolls, but real persons, who have feelings, emotions, and needs to reconnect those *shot line crossings to each other's bows.* We are, after all, and always will be, *SHIPMATES, in LEADERSHIP!*

AUTHOR BIO

FORCM (SW)
THOMAS J. SNEE,
USN, (RET), M.ED

Thomas J. (Tom) Snee stepped down as the Twelfth National Executive Director, for Fleet Reserve Association (FRA), Alexandria, VA, in December 2019. During his term in office, he represented over 45,000 Sea Service personnel and their families on various boards and congressional committees for military and Veterans benefits. He has since returned to teaching, to motivate and inspire Middle and High School students in the Northern Virginia area. He is continually active with his Church, Boy Scouts, and other Youth Groups.

Mr. Snee is a retired Navy Master Chief /Surface Warfare Specialist, with over 30 years of naval service and a Vietnam Veteran. He has testified before the House, Senate and Veterans, Congressional Committees for personnel and operational issues. He served as a panel member on the Senate Congressional Educational Reform for Educators. A champion for military and family benefits, he is a passionate person mentor, who continues to *spearhead* many key initiatives for our military within the Departments of Defense, Homeland Security, and Veteran Administration.

A Cleveland, Ohio native, Tom grew up and graduated in 1965 from Willoughby South High School, Willoughby, OH. He is an Eagle Scout, was a morning newspaper carrier for **The Cleveland Plain Dealer,** and a summer playground supervisor/counselor. He serves on many leadership positions with the Boy Scouts of America throughout the numerous locations he has lived. He is currently with local Boy Scout Troops in the Northern Virginia area.

After graduating from high school, Tom enlisted in the United States Navy. He initially served as a Yeoman however, converted to the Navy Counselor field. He served as the Force Master Chief, Navy Recruiting Command, Washington, DC; Command Master Chief onboard USS AMERICA (CV-66) and at Navy Recruiting District, Chicago, IL. He was the Curriculum Director/Course Supervisor for the Chief of Naval Technical Training, Millington, TN and Program Manager for the Chief of Naval Personnel Command, Washington, DC, for Senior Enlisted Development. As course supervisor, he, and his team, developed measurable standards to reduce student attrition and significant monetary expenditures throughout the U. S. Navy's training commands. He also has served on major sea, shore and staff commands and is a graduate of the Navy's Senior Enlisted Academy, Class 009/Khaki, Naval War College, Newport, RI.

Following his Navy retirement, Tom worked for the FRA as a Veterans Service Officer and Membership/Branch Development Coordinator. In August of 2000, he transitioned careers and taught Middle

School and was an Administrator, in the Arlington VA Diocese. He currently serves on the Commonwealth of Virginia's Catholic Schools Certification, **Designed for Excellence** (DFE) Teams. As a Middle School teacher, he taught Religion, American History, Government, Geography, and Economics. He is also a Confirmation CCD 8th grade teacher.

Mr. Snee is a member of the FRA, Knights of Columbus, Surface Navy Association (SNA) and National Eagle Scout Association (NESA). His numerous citations and accolades are especially noteworthy from the **WHO's WHO** circuits which include: **"Worldwide Leadership and Achievement in Industry and Professionalism; American Teachers; Business Professional; Executive of the Year Award 2018-2019; 2019 Lifetime and American Achievement Award; The American Achievement Award for 2018; Eagle Award as the Top Male Entrepreneur for 2018;"** and **'Teacher of the Year, for 2011'**. In 1997 he was inducted into the **"Distinguish Alumni Hall of Fame Award"** for the Willoughby-Eastlake Ohio Schools. In 2021 & 2018 he was name in the **"Top 100 Registry for Business Leaders and Professionals Lifetime Achievement for Veteran Affairs, Man of the Year and Military Leadership Award"**. In December 2018, was named the **"2018 Top National Executive Director"**, and in 2022 named as the **"The Lifetime Achievement Award"** from the International Association of Top Professionals, (IAOTP).

Mr. Snee holds an M.Ed, in Education Leadership, from George Mason University, Fairfax, VA, and a BS, in Liberal Arts/Psychology from Excelsior College, Albany, NY. In 2016 he was bestowed an Honorary Degree for **Alumni Services,** from Excelsior College and delivered their 2021 Commencement Address. In 2019 he was awarded the **'College of Education and Human Development (CEHD) Distinguished Alumni Award'** from George Mason University and delivered their Commencement Address.

Mr. Snee continues to serve on many boards including at Excelsior College, Albany, NY; Surface Navy Association; and Mount Vernon/ Gunston Hall. He is an author of two books: **"What's Up, Life"** and, **"You Raise Me Up."** His third book, **'Leadership: Reaching Out,**

Pulling Up, Holding On, To Stand Strong Together,' is due out in 2022.

Mr. Snee was married to the late Karen A. Habina for 46 years, who also was from Willoughby, OH. The Snee's have four children: Janet Basselgia, Springfield, VA, an elementary school teacher and STEM Coordinator, Burke, VA; Denise McCready, Goose Greek, SC, Special Ed; David, a U. S. Navy Captain, Tampa, FL; and Timothy, of Woodbridge, VA, with FedEx. They have seven grandchildren, and he currently resides in Burke, VA.

Tom's life has been noted with many professional "footnotes." One bestowed by parents and students alike is from Robert H. Shaffer: *"We must never view young people as empty bottles to be filled, but as candles to be lit*." His favorites are: *"It's always too soon to quit"* and, *"Output is the optimum of any total commitment and involvement"*! He personally coined the phrases: *"I am but a Humble Servant for the Success of Others;" "Listen, Lead, Love, Let Go, Mentor, Coach, and then Manage;" "Inclusion is the 'cornerstone' to saying YES"; "We must be SILENT, and LISTEN, to Everyone," "Say Yes to One's Potential"* and, *"I dare You, don't just FINISH, keep STARTING."*

www.ingramcontent.com/pod-product-compliance
Lightning Source LLC
Chambersburg PA
CBHW022019150726

47990CB00002B/723